THE LIBRARY
ST. MARY'S COLLEGE OF MARYLAND
ST. MARY'S CITY, MARYLAND 20686

VALUABLE NAIL

FIELD TRANSLATION SERIES 5

D1522031

Günter Eich

VALUABLE NAIL
SELECTED POEMS

Translated by Stuart Friebert,
David Walker, and David Young

Introduction by David Young

FIELD Translation Series 5

Many of these translations have appeared in the following journals: *Antaeus*, *Field*, *Iowa Review*, *Ironwood*, *Malahat Review*, *Quarterly Review of Literature*.

Special thanks to Suhrkamp Verlag/Frankfurt and Ilse Aichinger for permission to use these poems.

Publication of this book was made possible through grants from the Ohio Arts Council and Laurence Perrine.

Copyright © 1981 by Oberlin College

Library of Congress Cataloging in Publication Data
   Eich, Günter (translated by Stuart Friebert, David
   Walker, and David Young)
     VALUABLE NAIL
     (The FIELD Translation Series; v. 5)
LC: 80-85332
ISBN: 0-932440-08-8
     0-932440-09-6 (paperback)

CONTENTS

INTRODUCTION
by David Young

In the summer of 1966, Stuart Friebert and I traveled to Europe on an H. H. Powers Grant to meet with a number of West German poets. Translation was one of our aims, along with an anthology of contemporary German poetry. While the anthology was eventually shelved, the translations flourished, and the whole trip was valuable in ways that are still making themselves felt. We met a number of distinguished writers—among them Günter Grass, Karl Krolow, Paul Celan, Rainer Brambach, Helmut Heissenbüttel, and Hilde Domin—and had a chance to compare their literary culture with ours in some detail. The meeting that impressed us both the most took place in a small village in the Bavarian Alps, near the German-Austrian border; it was with Günter Eich and his wife, the writer Ilse Aichinger. We had already begun our translations of Eich's poems, and this encounter spurred our efforts. Eich had just published a rich and powerful collection of poems, *Anlässe und Steingärten*, and we were excited by the discovery of a major writer who was still so little known outside his own country. In the next few years Eich's collections of prose poems appeared, and as we worked to cope with their challenges we found one of our own students, David Walker (already a FIELD editor as an undergraduate and now a colleague), who had the necessary gifts and interest to translate them effectively. Thus was the trio of translators responsible for the present volume brought together in a shared enterprise of enthusiasm and mutual support. All the translations collected here have benefited from the ideas and suggestions of all three translators, although there is a principal translator in each case, identified in the note that follows this introduction.

Our conversations with Günter Eich (Stuart Friebert returned for second and third visits in 1968 and 1970), as well as our subsequent correspondence, centered on the poetry, not on the life. We knew vaguely that he had fought on the Russian front during the war and had been a prisoner of war briefly in a camp in the United States, and that his career as a poet had really begun significantly in the postwar period, when he and a group of like-minded writers, the Group 47, had tried to forge an aesthetic appropriate to postwar Germany; but Eich was rather reticent, both as a poet and as an individual, about the misfortunes and details of his own history. The chronology appended to the introduction outlines his life, but our emphasis here, as he would have wanted, must be on his accomplishments as a writer of lyric poems and of radio plays, arguably the most important figure in both areas that Germany has produced since World War II.

Any consideration of Günter Eich's importance as a poet must take into account the postwar situation in Germany, where writers found a common purpose in the effort to reconstitute their language as an instrument of knowledge and truth. They formed a generation with a special sense of the precarious and invaluable nature of language, its necessity, its incredible abuses, its rare moments of precision and imaginative perfection. Paul Celan spoke of the German language having to "pass through its own unresponsiveness, pass through its own fearful muting, pass through the thousand darknesses of death-bringing speech." And Hans Magnus Enzensberger, a younger member of that postwar generation of poets, has testified to Eich's role in the difficult struggle that brought an end to the "fearful muting," a role that gave him a special esteem among his contemporaries:

After the entry of the Allies, Germany was mute, in the most precise meaning of the word, a speechless country. There is a poem in which this paralysis has itself become language, and which simultaneously describes and overcomes the situation; it has become famous and is regarded today as the birth certificate of the New German literature. Günter Eich wrote it: *Inventory* . . . Eich's poem is as quiet as it is radical. It is written from the situation of a prisoner of war in a camp; but this situation simultaneously stood for the condition of all Germans. The poet is staking a claim to the absolute minimum that remains; to a material, spiritual, and linguistic remnant. His manner of writing corresponds to this. It is stripped down as far as poetry can be stripped. The text sounds like a man learning to speak; it is with such elementary sentences that language courses begin. This was the position of German literature after the war: it had to learn its own language.

Eich's subsequent development was an expansion, never an abandonment, of the "elementary" quality of "Inventory." His poetry—not to mention his remarkable late prose poems—has great variety and imaginative daring, as the present selection shows. But the "minimum," the claim staked to shreds and remnants, to the things we begin to notice and prize when our dignity and comfort are stripped away, like the "valuable nail" in "Inventory," remains a central characteristic of his aesthetic, his way of thought and life. "A Mixture of Routes," one of his finest poems, ends:

A moment of comfort drawn from barracks,
from rotting grass, rotting ropes.

Asked what that meant, Eich replied, "Comfort comes only from rotting grass, not from philosophy." Why "rotting"? Well, the barracks belong to a former concentration camp, and the moment of comfort is simply that they are no longer put to that use. Evil rots and passes too— a dour kind of solacing. That this tentative and skeptical approach to experience was also the basis for Eich's attitude toward language is made clear in his fine essay, "Some Remarks on 'Literature and Reality,' " appended to this collection.

To say that Eich was a poet who had to recreate and revalidate a language for poetry is not, however, to deny him a tradition. At least three traditions converge in his work. There is first a clear link with German romanticism, especially in its tendency to find mysterious signs and tokens in the natural world. In a comparatively early poem—not included here—a stranger looks at the leg of a banded bird and reads the message with astonishment. In the same volume (titled, incidentally, *Botschaften des Regens*: messages or bulletins from the rain) the speaker of "Insight" confesses to a sort of paranoia—Mexico is an invented country because he has never been there—but finds truth hidden in his kitchen cupboard, in labeled canisters. Later poems, like "Half," find a wistful speaker passing a token to someone else, "But / I give you a snail to take, / that will keep a long time." Eich plays with and even parodies the tradition, but it is obviously one that attracts his imagination. In a post-Auschwitz world he reads nature's hieroglyphs with caution, even distrust; still, the notion that the world of objects, studied carefully, has mysteries to reveal and saving strengths to put one's faith in, persists and prospers when it can.

A second tradition is that of Chinese poetry. As a young man before the war, Eich studied to be a Sinologist, and his explorations of the Chinese poetic tradition, which included a good deal of translating, left their mark. If he is less portentous than romantic poets, more cool and direct and natural, he owes that in part to the

Chinese manner of simple images simply presented, taking their meanings from juxtaposition and implication, with little or no accompanying comment. His mastery of the idiom and techniques of Chinese poetry remained a constant and valuable background to all his writing.

There is also good reason for linking Eich's poetry with the European poetry of this century that is called "hermetic." This term often seems to spread more confusion than clarity, but if we lack its precise definition we have some notion of its dimensions: associations with such poets as Char, Celan, Ungaretti, and Sandor Weores, and, swinging a wider arc, elements in the work of poets as diverse as Mandelstam, Vallejo, and Yeats; a tendency not only toward a private manner and vocabulary but toward condensation as well—a clipped, pithy, hard-edged manner; an inwardness that has little to do with the extravagant means of the surrealists; and a kind of tough-mindedness that seems to insist that lyrics must be chipped and carved from the roughest materials and with the simplest tools. Seen in light of this tradition, Eich's work makes sense not only in individual poems but in its development, for more and more it acquires a wry, self-contained, and undoubtedly difficult manner that is also the source of an exhilarating music. We might say that a good hermetic poet, like a good hermit, is learning to talk (or sing) to himself or herself (as opposed, say, to a confessional poet, who is presumably anxious to talk *to* someone), and that his or her aim must be first and foremost to avoid the garrulous. Thus Eich's poems grow harder and denser and, if we accept their direction, lovelier. Instead of "messages from the rain" we have by 1966, *Anlässe und Steingärten*: occasions and rock gardens. The Japanese *ryoanji* referred to in that title make an appropriate metaphor for the poetry—spare of means but yielding much to study and meditation, mysterious but simple, hard but astonishingly graceful. Yet it also seems clear that Eich more or less backed himself into a corner by letting his hermetic tendency run its course: it is hard to imagine him going much further in the directions represented by the 1966 volume, and easy to see that, in order to avoid disappearing from sight or becoming so dry and dense no reader could follow him, it was natural for him to change his medium to prose and his manner to that of *Maulwürfe* (moles). The prose poems are scarcely a repudiation of Eich's hermeticism, but they represent a release, a burrowing out from under that corner. At any rate, if the concept of hermetic poetry continues to be an interesting and helpful way of seeing a great deal of twentieth-century European poetry, then Eich deserves recognition as a major practitioner.

When we have seen Eich as a distinguished member of a literary generation struggling to reconstitute a language, and as a poet whose work combines three traditions—romantic, Chinese, and hermetic—with distinctive results, we are closer to understanding his importance and uniqueness. But a further step remains, that of comprehending Eich's imaginative freedom, always a miracle but especially miraculous in the circumstances in which his identity as a writer was fashioned. For if the problem of being truly imaginative is a universal hurdle for the poet, and can be seen in universal terms, it often makes the most sense to see it in terms of the poet's time and place. Thus Hopkins, for example, is more acutely understood when his accomplishment is presented in terms of his effort to break free of Victorian sensibilities and, more especially, the worst tendencies of Victorian poetry. This problem, for Eich, was posed not by the war or its aftermath, but by the dangerous sameness with which writers responded to it. Here we must acknowledge the moralistic tendencies of German postwar poetry; one is sympathetic to the writer's need to present credentials that reassure the reader as to matters of social conscience and political concern, but the results are too often dismaying and dull. The influence of Brecht, an easy and safe model for poetry of this kind, has not been a happy one, as anyone who reads through the reams of poetry produced after his manner will come to recognize. And the challenge for a major poet in these circumstances lies in the ability to transcend, without altogether abandoning, the impulse to moralistic and political poems with predictable, earnest sentiments.

Without attempting to assess the achievement of any other poet, one can point to Eich's remarkable success in combining responsibility and freedom. The best test will come in reading the poems, but two guideposts may be useful. The metaphor of travel that is not travel is surely one of the most significant in Eich's poetry, for it expresses the combination of moral responsibility—staying home and facing the past —and of imaginative freedom—the poet's eternal privilege—that Eich's poetry achieves at its best. Here travel must be understood in its full variety of possibilities—taking a walk, hurtling around the world in an airplane, letting one's mind wander, visiting an alien Japan which turns out to be a strange mirror of Germany—for an appreciation of the way the metaphor works and of the fact that it succeeds precisely because it is metaphor, a way of stating the condition that transcends the prosaic. Similarly, we may find another useful guide to Eich's achievement in his use of what might be called a "glancing" technique: subjects brush past rapidly, issues are seen at the edge of the vision, two or three words make up a concise image that must stand for a great chunk of terrible history. Hence the "postcards," hasty scribbles of the imagination; hence poems like "Lemberg" (the German name for the Russian city of Lvovsk), where one or two characteristics—the sound of the name, the terminus of the streetcar line—suggest, like the tip of an iceberg, meanings that Germany and Russia have for each other after wars, after years, after the deadening weight of hatred and suffering. Eich worked at first in short poems, where this "glancing" technique was almost a necessity; then, as he gained confidence and command, he was able to use it consistently in longer poems and sustained sequences. Poems like "Brickworks Between 1900 and 1910," "Seminar for Survivors," "Ryo-anji," and, perhaps to excess, the enigmatic "Continuing the Conversation," remain, for this reason, among the most remarkable achievements of the poet's canon. They brought down charges of unnecessary difficulty and irresponsibility on Eich's head, as did the prose poems, but they will endure when the reams and reams of righteous, simplistic poems after the manner of Brecht have been forgotten.

All this is not to claim that Eich is without limits or faults. Some of his poems are trivial, others are predictable; at times his way of muttering to himself about clearly private associations can be exasperating. But this selection is designed to show the poet at his best. It does not exhibit the early poems very thoroughly. And it de-emphasizes chronology in order to illustrate the consistency of the poet's imagination and to refute the charges that the prose poems were an uncharacteristic and irresponsible falling-off. If it succeeds in some of these aims it may not only introduce Eich to English and American readers whose acquaintance with his work is long overdue; it may clarify his position for his own countrymen.

•

A NOTE ON THE TRANSLATIONS

All the translations in this volume are in a sense collaborations, since the editors worked closely together on each poem. The following list identifies the principal translator of each poem. Katherine Bradley translated two poems while a student at Oberlin.

From *Abgelegene Gehöfte* (1948): Inventory (translated by David Young)

From *Botschaften des Regens* (1955): Insight, Days with Jays, Where I Live, Lemberg, End of August, Abandoned Mountain Pasture, Brook in December (translated by David Young)

From *Zu den Akten* (1964): Quotation from Norway, Munch, Consul Sandberg (translated by David Young); Too Late for Modesty, Remainder, For Example, Old Postcards (1), New Postcards (1), Talks That Never Take Place (translated by Stuart Friebert); Carrying Bag (translated by David Walker)

From *Anlässe und Steingärten* (1966): Widely Travelled, Smokebeer, A Mixture of Routes, Learning About the Landscape, Half, Ryoanji, Seminar for Backward Pupils, Definitive, Timetable, Brickworks Between 1900 and 1910, Geometrical Place, Continuing the Conver-

sation (translated by David Young); Old Post-
cards (2), Berlin 1918 (translated by Katherine
Bradley); New Postcards (2), Little Daughter
(translated by Stuart Friebert)

From *Maulwürfe* (1968): Preamble (translated by
Stuart Friebert); Sin (translated by John Lynch
and David Young); Winter Student and
Daughter-Son, Nathanael, Cure, Seahorses,
Salt, Late June Early July, Change of Cli-
mate, Marketplace, A Day in Okayama,
Viareggio (translated by David Walker)

From *Ein Tibeter in meinem Büro* (1970): Magic
Spells (translated by Stuart Friebert); Carsten-
sen, Lauras, Key Figure, Repeating Dictionary,
Beethoven, Wolf, and Schubert (translated by
David Walker)

"Some Remarks on 'Literature and Reality' "
was translated by Stuart Friebert.

A GÜNTER EICH CHRONOLOGY

1907: Born in Lebus on the Oder river.

1918: Moves to Berlin (with family).

1925: Completes his "Abitur" (high school diploma) in Leipzig, after which he immediately begins Sinology studies in Berlin.

1927: First poems published, under pseudonym Erich Günter, in *Anthologie jüngster Lyrik* (edited by Klaus Mann and Willi Fehse).

1929: First radio play is performed, *Das Leben und Sterben des Sängers Caruso*, written in collaboration with Martin Raschke.

1929-30: A year of study in Paris, because, in his words, "there were no courses in Sinology in Germany that year."

1930: First volume of poems appears, *Gedichte* (Jess Publishers, Dresden).

1932: Joins the circle of writers known as *Kolonne*.

1933: Back to Berlin.

1933-39: Works in radio. Writes no poems.

1939-45: Serves as a soldier in World War II.

1945-46: Prisoner of war; begins writing poems again.

1946: Released from captivity, returns to Greisenhausen to pick up his life again.

1947: Founding member of the Gruppe 47.

1948: First major collection appears, *Abgelegene Gehöfte*.

1949: Another volume of poems appears, *Untergrundbahn*.

1950-59: Most productive radio and puppet play period.

1950: His radio play, *Geh nicht nach El Kuwehd* is performed; receives the Gruppe 47 Prize.

1951: Bavarian Academy literary prize.

1952: Prize for radio plays.

1953: Marries Ilse Aichinger and makes his home in Lenggries in Oberbayern.

1955: His collection *Botschaften des Regens* appears; becomes a member of Bavarian Academy of the Arts.

1959: Georg Büchner Prize.

1964: *Zu den Akten* (poems) appears.

1966: *Anlässe und Steingärten* (poems).

1968: Prose sketches appear, *Maulwürfe*; Schiller Prize.

1970: More prose sketches, *Ein Tibeter in meinem Büro*.

1972: Eich's death.

A MIXTURE OF ROUTES

1
The forests in the glove compartment,
random cities,
promise of food and lodging.

My cortisone face
shoved across pastures,
my electroshock,
my cozy motel.

Unnatural pleasures
happily practiced,
having lived with
the wise ciphers of the timetable,
on my mapped tongue I keep
these lands for my own.

2

Ach: that is aqua
and it's a sigh.
Go into the seas!

Get, unwittingly,
to Kagoshima,
the first city,

unwittingly to the sighs
of asylum doors,
the waters around tanneries,

fishkitchens
south of the Main,
the peevish, red

parking lights,
a dateline
in Obergries,

a sixth-form
gym class,
a farewell ball

with the girl named Tabe
and the elevator girls

whom nobody looks at,

get there
to say Adieu
get to stationery stores and

a middlesized ferryboat.

3

Finally the doors are closed,
the taps shut off,
ashes in the oven, nothing left,
we can go.

Always the narrow passes, the snow tongues,
where are the roses of the teacher,
the rain-animals through broken windows,
the movie programs through the letter-slot
on Thursdays.

Where are, after the snow tongues,
after Thursdays, our
ways? Into the forest toward Hiroshima,
between dogs the stairs in the quarry,
a moment of comfort drawn from barracks,
from rotting grass, rotting ropes.

WIDELY TRAVELLED

Just beyond Vancouver
the forest starts,
nothing starts,
whatever we fly over
starts.

Everything northern, the way you like it,
a salt grain for whoever runs in the forest,
leather pouches, possibly
for gunpowder, spices, tobacco.

Whatever starts goes very far,
a column of smoke from the Böhmerwald,
a perspective, there are
few people.

TIMETABLE

These airplanes
between Boston and Düsseldorf.
Pronouncing judgments
is hippopotamus business.
I prefer
putting lettuce leaves
on a sandwich and
staying wrong.

VIAREGGIO

I was in Viareggio relatively often, seven or eight times, more often than Munich, less often than Antwerp. I grew up in Antwerp, it's famous for something I've forgotten, maybe frogs legs. If it's frogs legs, then they're exported, and the Antwerpers chew legless frogs, sullenly. But as I said, I could be wrong, perhaps it's fallow deer or carrier pigeons; at any rate, it had something to do with nature, if my youthful memories don't deceive me.

I was in Munich only once, just passing through, twenty minutes. I associate it with the taste of a certain lemonade. I don't know whether I was there as child or grandfather, in any case it was long ago.

But now Viareggio itself. It lies in Galicia, just over the Portuguese border, and is famous for its football team, the Black and Reds, who have already defeated, for example, Lokomotive-Karlmarxstadt several times, the last time it was even one to nothing.

From Viareggio I received a card with the football team, black and red, but I suspect that only the postmark is genuine. That's how I come to the real subject, the connections, the background, the suspicion, I'm not even sure whether it's a football team or fieldmice. Everything's possible, if the television is focused, you recognize the better things in Viareggio and elsewhere, especially at night in the lamplight, where no one watches, and let's not talk about the graveyards. And the folklore about legs, which, on the other hand, only the whistle of a distant locomotive can help you forget, from Karlmarxstadt or Antwerp—let's be cross and find the one no better than the other.

But Viareggio, I was there often, seven or eight times, maybe closer to seven, but I was.

OLD POSTCARDS

1

Here's where I wanted to put the streetcars
and swing
on the chain around the war memorial.
A sign for the deaf and dumb.
A sermon for the bakers
lolling about in the morning wind.

2

The view, gradually
colored by glue,
leaf cover and road
all cut
by the same knife.
The asphalting planned
like dying.

3

Two kinds of handwriting—
a bicycle trip
to the castle ruins.
But we're okay.
Playing in the black sand.
Chewing bread
for the holes in the wallpaper.

4

Blowtube on Sedan Day,
three zero four,
it's red in the lime trees.
Tomorrow tomorrow tomorrow.

5

Hold tight
to the tanners' ropes
till the angels come
with their huge caps and shoulder cloth,
according to evidence of the stones,
the print in the smoke
you can trust.

6

Tell me something
from the catalogues,
and where you've been so long,
about the stamps in the beehive,
our grandfathers' professions
and the smell of hooves.
I'll count the drops for you
on the sugar,
a prime number,
and I'll eat with you.

7

Paris,
which reminds me of
Mexican hats,
ribbons
with the steps of lovers,
information booths and mustard seeds.

8

There are
no cranes here.
But there are women
and races and
a laugh to keep you pondering,
old as
Renaissance staircases,
the steps of the prisoners
going down.

9

We're among the last.
To our left someone who
knew caves left yesterday.
Our preserves are all gone.
I was thinking, even yesterday,
of the oil jugs of the crusaders,

handed over to their besiegers,
honorably,
of the rain.

10

Why the coffee
wasn't drunk?
Well we were sitting okay
right down in the flooded parts,
our rented boats
between the boulevard trees.
Why the sugar
wouldn't dissolve?
Nothing ever ended.
Here's what still needs
telling: the cups, a
Charlotte who was taking our money, her
sad ruffles wet through and through.

11

Fine,
fine.
But when the war is over
we'll go to Minsk
and pick up Grandmother.

QUOTATION FROM NORWAY

We continue to think
the grass on the rooftops,
leave the fjords to the left,
partisans of the fog.
Where can you cry
in this country?
The lemmings
have gone into the sea.
The tobacco pouches
of polar explorers
preserve Time
in little crumbs.

SALT

A music historian explains the monkeybread tree to us—which is, on the whole, always the case. We aren't surprised, we're used to ethnology and the study of customs, but we drink beer to get over it. History drinks water when it's thirsty. Those are the differences, we're proud of it.

No short Sundays, no obligations in the evenings. No, we stay on the steps of the mission school, between the mussels. There's a place with a view of the wooden bridge, the cemetery that's worth seeing, the black pigs with sharp snouts. Here the world begins. A transparent classroom, a green umbrella blowing toward us from the sea. The corrugated iron doors are closed at night and noon. We're walking, we're going, are we going away? Anyway, the crested larks will stay behind. We're going because we long to be naturalized in the country of Hsin, to fill woven baskets with salt, to wither away in salt gardens.

They certainly need salt. But longings?

BERLIN 1918

The majority between Zoo,
Potsdam Station, Molken Market,
the Kaiser and the Spanish flu,
happenings and confections,
a dead face in the pillows, October,
all there is to know about bed bugs,
all about the waiter, Albert, the sad
trips to the country, and always
the missing connections,
the children's hours at the kitchen sink,
everything nouns, the flu,
Otto the Hunter, the Kaiser, everything
between Holzmarkt Street and
Landwehrkanal, November.

LEMBERG

1

City on how many hills.
Graying yellow.
A bell sound accompanies you,
audible in the clank
of your identity tag.

2

Slopes like fear, unfathomable.
The streetcar line ends
on a weedy steppe
before worn doors.

INVENTORY

This is my cap,
this is my coat,
here's my shaving gear
in a linen sack.

A can of rations:
my plate, my cup,
I've scratched my name
in the tin.

Scratched it with this
valuable nail
which I hide
from avid eyes.

In the foodsack is
a pair of wool socks
and something else that I
show to no one,

it all serves as a pillow
for my head at night.
The cardboard here lies
between me and the earth.

The lead in my pencil
I love most of all:
in the daytime it writes down
the verses I make at night.

This is my notebook,
this is my tarpaulin,
this is my towel,
this is my thread.

CURE

Too cool for the season, too awake for the hour. You hear the time-signal, once again you hear the stones underfoot, then the swamps begin. The road over the pass is blocked by a mule. Mules are rare here, they are military mules.

Through binoculars you recognize the patients in the valley, on the way to their painful treatments at the barracks-yard of a company that has just arrived, mute, a gray slide. Several rice farmers are still breathing underwater, but don't worry, the machine guns are trained on the most important points. You dear ones, weren't we in Karlsbad just now, Abano, Reichenhall? Continue your treatments peacefully, we are well-protected, your treatments take place between the lines, between the lines of Chinese poems, time passes so quickly, the season, so short the road to Tinchebray, the lines so narrow.

SEMINAR FOR BACKWARD PUPILS

1

While the dead
cool quickly
a slow waltz
for the S.P.D.

Enough of rose bouquets
for the proper occasion,
speak finally of
crumpled print
and the goulash
foolishly spilled
on striped trousers.

We need a
patriotic stay-at-home zither
for five places
in a realistically designed
government bunker.

2

Then came
mustard-skilled men,
turnip counters,
delegates of welfare.

Wooden eye, be watchful!

They scoured us clean
with sandpaper,
factual accounts
and politeness.

Wooden eye, be watchful!

Now we know everything:
the sun lies always before us.
We define freedom anew:
soon
we'll be rid of it.

Wooden eye.

3

We crossed
the frontier of a hundred boots
and my memory went into action,
the letters from A to Z
occurred to me
and the numbers almost to one hundred,
my abilities
boot, heel and toe.
And I decided
to take service
in the dungeons of justice.

HALF

Between cabbage leaves
grows the ceremonious
poppy hour,
a sandy love,
that emigrates.
Go! The preserves
are fermenting on the shelves,
we can
gather spiderwebs
along the canal
and carry off, unseen,
a pocketful of sand
from the construction site,
we could, if
there were no fences,
go cross country to
Amsterdam.

But
I give you a snail to take,
that will keep a long time.

END OF AUGUST

With white bellies the dead fish hang
among duckweed and bulrushes.
The crows have wings, to fly away from death.
Sometimes I know that God
cares most about the existence of the snail.
He builds her a house. Us
he does not love.

Evening: the bus drags
a white banner of dust
as it brings home the soccer team.
The moon glows among willows
reconciled with the evening star.
How near you are, Immortality,
in the wing of a bat,
in the eyes of those headlights
coming down the hill.

BROOK IN DECEMBER

1

The green crests of water plants
combed by the current
across the forehead of the stone.
Ideas
make the water icy.

2

The lines of the ice-rim sketch unrest,
the fever of reeds, the earthquake of snails.
Their diagrams are waited for.

3

The oil slick went downstream like a boat,
the fishing rod's shadow is forgotten.
Current, insight of the fish—

LEARNING ABOUT THE LANDSCAPE

I know
one of the rare, dry
riverbeds,
my brother knows it,
my deaf mother.

There's nothing to hear,
no family
connections, no
excuses, no wisdom.

Dry riverbeds are
geological and a life support,
don't grieve for the fossils,
don't sleep on the heart side.

And so they are useful to us
as camomile is useful,
sideways along the hill
and to be taken in drops,
like dew.

SEAHORSES

Our surroundings are imprecise, we have the sun inside, an old categorical imperative of Immanuel Kant. Immanuel had no children, too bad. Menzel didn't have any either, or Gottfried Keller. Maybe everything would have been different, if they had been seahorses, the imperative less categorical, the glue less important. But that couldn't have been demanded then. In seahorses the eggs are the critical factor. See, there are other ways, even parthenogenesis.

I'm always confusing nature with mountain views. But never mind, even at two thousand meters it's categorical and imperative. There's no literature there. No chance of changing the world, in any event, landslides, volcanic eruptions, and crosses at the summit with books for entering your consent. Dated. For conservative hearts. The others take the bus.

Ah, ah, ah, so many sighs, so many dates. How many women have you had, how many men? Did they lie in the spruce needles or in the bus? Did they study political science later or monochromatic painting, no more distinctions, mouse-gray.

But we will push biology ahead. Though my sex is male, I think I'm pregnant. Not long ago I thought I was avant garde, that's how you get specialists. My andrologist was talking about a Caesarean, but they're still so oldfashioned. I'd been thinking about Zeus.

DAYS WITH JAYS

The jay does not throw me
its blue feather.

The acorns of his shrieks
grind in the early dawn.
A bitter flour, food
for the whole day.

All day, behind red leaves,
with a hard break
he hacks the night
out of branches, seeds, nuts,
a cloth that he pulls over me.

His flight is like a heartbeat.
But where does he sleep
and what is his sleep like?
The feather lies by my shoe
unseen in the darkness.

ABANDONED MOUNTAIN PASTURE

Rainwater
in the hoofprints of cattle.
Helpless flies
close to November.

The red nail will not withstand the wind.
The shutter will screech on its hinges,
sometimes hitting the casement,
sometimes the wall.

Who will hear it?

LATE JUNE EARLY JULY

A summer day, the beekeeping's going well, pears thrive for the faithful, a day when it's a question of ichneumon flies.

The old question still darkens the wheat, and the utopias pass by crooked. The oak leaves are rounded and the aspen leaves are sharp, you sob in admiration. You can still produce dreams from the wheat fungus, an alcohol stove is all you need. We go out and praise and trust our pork-butcher because he uses mild seasoning. The question of cats between easy chair and lilac bush, the terrible summer day, so much more beautiful than Solomon's silk.

The tapered veils, Spanish mantillas, the garotte, machine guns, trials, stewards, one turns into the next, practical and all in tune, the hunger and the costs, the question of people, shouted, whispered, unthought, photographed and recorded on tapes, all one summer day in the Baroque of Paul Gerhardt. Badminton and underwater hunting are added, but the blood is revolutionary conservative red regardless of skin color, the question of people, accepted politically, a beautiful summer day.

SMOKEBEER

Pretzelsellers and deafmutes,
my headlines,
that crouch in the passageway
over a communal beer.

I stare at their conversations,
their modest
and everlasting horror,
my headlines,
my Kennedys,
my Khruschevs.

CONTINUING THE CONVERSATION

1

Remembering the dead man
I observed
that remembering is a form of forgetting.

It said:
rescue the flames from the ashes,
pursue Geology in the discarded
sediment of the instant,
restore the time sequence
from the insoluble chemistry.

It said:
separate the critique of birdflight
from the morning shopping
and the expectation of love.
Proceed to where
the parallels cross.
Fulfill the demands of logic
by means of dreams.
Take the fossils from their cases,
thaw them with the warmth of your blood.
Seek the sign
instead of the metaphor
and thereby the only place
where you are, always.
I move along
in order to translate anthills,
to taste tea with a closed mouth,
to slice tomatoes
under the salt of the verses.

2

Invite him over

The shame, that the survivor is right,
exempt from sentencing
and with the arrogance of judgment!

Who denies
that green things are green?
That lends our word
a lovely security,
the significance of a solid base.
But the stylizing
that the heart
imposes on itself
keeps its motives
like the ammonite
the dead man looks at.
It wants to extend feelers,
turn vine-leaves into fernspirals,
bring errors into blossom,
hear autumn as a whiff of snow.

But don't forget the houses
in which you live among us.
The lounge chair in the garden
will suit you
or the view of trees through the window
that makes you prop
your elbows on your knees.
Come in out of the rain, and speak!

3

Converse with him

Here it began and it didn't begin,
here it continues
in a noise from the next room,
in the click of the switch,
in shoes taken off behind the door.
The pallor of your face
that blots out colors
isn't valid now.
Sentences come from habits
that we scarcely noticed.
The way the necktie's tied
is a momentous objection,
the ability to fall asleep quickly
a proof against subjective interpretations,
the preference for tea
classifies the existence of animals.

4

Find his theme

Interchangeable:
the knocking at the door
which began the conversation
and the waving
as the streetcar clanged,

the name on the grave cross
and the name on the garden gate,
children grown up
and postcard greetings from Ragusa.

Words as pulsations of air,
the organ note from the bellows,
the decision
to hear the song
or to be the song—
warped uprights
to the fall line of phosphorus,
when the theme begins.
No variations accepted
not the excuses of power
and the reassurances of truth,
use cunning
to track down the questions
behind the answer's broad back.

5

Reading his book and his death
Figures settled in
at the shut-down mines of Zinnwald
behind the demon frenzy
of subalpine slopes and season,

while the foreground
is occupied by ruffians
who divide our hours among themselves.

Pirna in balance with the Pyramids,
the freedom of express trains
cashed in small change by block leaders,
the family ethically founded,
contempt for nomads and loners.

But the objections
come back to the sentences
like eager adjectives,
a line of termites
that hollows them out
to a thin skin
of black letters.

The Style is Death,
the shot in the stomach,
white rose in a morphine dream,
jokes to amuse life,
salvos into a snowstorm.

6

Winning confidence from his life

While you share the thoughts,
direct the conversation by your death,
writing along on poems,
gathering pears
and viewing new landscapes
(but I finally
resisted garden work)
meanwhile
Simona stiffened
into a figure of stone,
her fabricated warmth
under the cold of tears.
She waits for the moss,
the injuries of rain,
vine shoots and birdshit.
She'll decay to be warmed
to a life that we want to share,
patience!

CARSTENSEN

In the afternoon someone wants to come who plays the combs. Maybe you'll learn something, just don't give up too soon, there's always enough time. The splinters of a bottle in the snow are green, of course there remains the question: who would come if they were blue? Green lets one turn into the other, the color into the combs, the someone into the snow, yesterday there were still liberties, but at night someone threw a schnapps bottle out the window.

Carstensen drove me, eleven marks fifty. Does he have horses or a motor vehicle? Well, you have to be there. You can't answer for yourself. Controlled by the nine orifices of the body, the need for sleep remains. All experience to the contrary, you expect to wake up in a different life, with different colors, different arts, or simply as a different person who goes on gladly and wholly irresponsibly. If things work out, he has canaries and green herrings with him.

Carstensen appeared ten twelve years ago, he's already driven that long. At first only on red brick streets and straight across the dunes, rubbertired, unavoidable, but he's not the one who plays the combs—by the way, I imagine it must have been awful. Carstensen is really someone else, just like God, who he knows even less. He reaches his destination, nothing more. Carstensen is someone in whose life you could wake up, the one with canaries and herrings. But he wouldn't allow it, he'd lose his temper at least. I'd never try it.

Carstensen drove me, a receipt for the fare. If only you're there. This afternoon someone's coming, you can't put him off, look at the green splinters. I find them beautiful, I find everything beautiful, maybe it's my nature or it's only to-day, but today it is. What color are the combs? Do tunes sound different on yellow green violet? I'd prefer them secco. (Probably yellow.)

TOO LATE FOR MODESTY

We took the house
and covered the windows,
had enough supplies in the cellar,
coal and oil,
hid death in ampules
between the folds in our skin.

Through the crack in the door we see the world:
a rooster with its head cut off,
running through the yard.

It's crushed our hopes.
We hang our bedsheets on the balconies
and surrender.

WHERE I LIVE

When I opened the window,
fish swam into the room,
herring. A whole school
seemed to be passing by.
They sported among the pear trees too.
But most of them
stayed in the forest,
above the nurseries and the gravel pits.

They are annoying. Still more annoying
are the sailors
(also higher ranks, coxswains, captains)
who frequently come to the open window
and ask for a light for their awful tobacco.

I'd like to move out.

GEOMETRICAL PLACE

We have sold our shadow,
it hangs on a wall in Hiroshima,
a transaction we knew nothing of,
from which, embarrassed, we rake in interest.

And, dear friends, drink my whiskey,
I won't be able to find the tavern any more,
where my bottle stands
with its monogram,
old proof of a clear conscience.

I didn't put my penny in the bank
when Christ was born
but I've seen the grandchildren
of dogs trained to herd people
on the hills near the Danube School,
and they stared at me.

And I want, like the people of Hiroshima,
to see no more burnt skin,
I want to drink and sing songs,
to sing for whiskey,
and to stroke the dogs, whose grandfathers
sprang at people
in quarries and barbed wire.

You, my shadow,
on the bank at Hiroshima,
I want to visit you with all the dogs
now and then
and drink to you
to the prosperity of our accounts.

The museum is being demolished,
in front of it
I will slip to you
behind your railing,
behind your smile—our cry for help—
and we'll suit each other again,
your shoes into mine
precise
to the second.

A DAY IN OKAYAMA

My wax paper umbrellas, my days, my view
out the window in the morning. Cold rice with
cold fish for breakfast, elevator girls whom
everyone ignores, a belch, continuing break-
fast. Okayama is storks, rather obtrusive, I mea-
sure off all garden paths according to the plan,
the porter doesn't understand me. My um-
brellas, my umbrella. I buy myself a watch, the
tallest Japanese woman in my life walks past,
two meters tall and high sandals besides, while
the watch must be wound four times a day, the
magic of numbers and my wax paper.

I won't grow any more, I'll remain 1.70 meters tall, an average character, and my suitcase is too heavy for my character. I go through my character with umbrellas that change every hour, the ark is worth seeing, the storks are on loan, have identification disks, but I don't recognize them. A parking lot for buses, school uniforms, I think: young railwaymen. That's better than a caption, sad wax paper, sorrowful rice, my watch has stopped.

It is unconsolable, but itself a consolation, I mumble in intervals. I don't know what is unconsolable, I am consolable, consolable with umbrellas, with paths in the park, with 1.70 meters. But I mumble. Maybe I'm thinking above all of my suitcase. It's slipped my mind, not everything takes place in the present tense.

RYOANJI

Smoke signals for friends,
a favorable day, windless,
from the northeast slope
I get a white answer.
I add pinetrees.

And now wall after wall
with theories of language,
wall after wall
my sadness coughs through gold teeth,
rain and wooden sandals
on the wooden corridors
dead ends everywhere, I find,
anxiously, in darkness,
my toes ponder
the darkness,

I'm sorry for myself,
I disagree with my toes
disagree with my sadness,
I miss the smoke signals,
old, black, and partial to me.
Now they don't come any more,
now it's night,
now the fire comes,
best of all and
worst of all.
I don't much like fire,
I don't much like smoke
and the same goes for breath.
I like coughing, sort of,
or spitting,
or the dark thoughts of illness,
of darkness.
Even cameras seem strange to me
and pinetrees in flowerpots.
I understand khaki fruit better
and howling Old Japanese
and the bowing at the end of the escalator
and the raw fish.

And a lot of sounds with "und,"
and all of them
treacherously heartbreaking,
I welcome you, heart,
welcome you, things that do the breaking,
maybe there will be
paper boats on the Kamo,
made of folded petitions,
that's it,
entrusted to the mud puddle
—so often sung about
so lacking in in-
fluence—
where they anchor and wait
for the sinking of the petitioners
and closing remarks.

In the evening
the fever in the infirmary beds goes up,
you learn some things there,
the evidence for some things
isn't valid,

withered leaves rustle
in the wastepaper basket,
the hedgehogs under the bushes,
almost silent,
live within easy access
to the prickly hide of my insights,
we rub them together
but only the moss moves,
not the world.
We exchange addresses,
we exchange
our personal pronouns,
we have so much in common,
sunrises,
the future till nineteen hundred and seven.
Then we'll practice breathing,
together,
from the instructions of Cheyne
and the instructions of Stokes,
that will pass the time nicely
with the snoring accompaniment
of our inmost thoughts.

If someone wants to
he can hang photos in the showcases,
tell anecdotes
or listen to them,
discuss the situation,
ornithology, penmanship,
above all Good Night.
A determined clan, we hold out
with our hedgehogs
at the critical moment,
and don't turn back
where what's happened is piling itself
in baskets, sacks, barrels,
a storehouse, open to everyone,
doors bang, footsteps echo,
we don't hear, we're deaf too,
our region is in free fall.
Bushes, darknesses, and infirmary beds,
we won't colonize anymore,
we'll teach our daughters and sons the hedgehog
    words
and stick to disorder,
our friends bungling at the world.

TALKS THAT NEVER TAKE PLACE

We modest translators
—say of timetables,
hair color, cloud formations—
what should we say to those
who agree
and read the originals
(Like the one
who read the oatgrains
in Eulenspiegel's books)

Faced with that much confidence
our sadness is windy
mixed with rain,
takes the roofs off,
falls on every smile,
incurable.

for Peter Huchel

FOR EXAMPLE

For example sailcloth.

Translating one word into one other word,
that takes in salt and tar
and is made of linen,
preserves the smell,
the laughter and the last breath,
red and white and orange,
time controls
and the godly martyr.

Sailcloth and none,
the question:
where's an interjection
as an answer.

Between Schöneberg
and the star cover
the mythical place
and stone of meadows.

Task, set
for the time after you're dead.

REPEATING DICTIONARY

Greetings, Vera Holubetz, former owner of my dictionary. A name in Sütterlin on the endpaper. German-Sütterlin and Sütterlin-German, a limited edition. Pear is Sadness. Vera is Holubetz. The languages are that different. I don't want to know what Sadness is, I don't know Vera Sadness. I don't know Vera Holubetz either, have no idea, don't want any, no certainties either. I'm satisfied with her greeting in Sütterlin. Sütterlin is a place in Styria. In Styria the farmers must be bald. They eat arsenic, which makes them cheerful. Harvest songs ring out, the women rake hay and the hay deserves it. And everyone speaks Sütterlin, an arsenic tongue.

Right at the book-cart I began to read, a real find. The dictionary is repeating, begins at Saba and ends with Negro Jazz. Unorthodox, even exotic, a lot of illuminating material. I hardly need any more light.

There's so much to move you there. Not just philologically, but also in a purely human way. Why did Vera sell the book? Has she strayed from Sütterlin? Did she need a little money for fruit bonbons? Was she more interested in technical drawings? Or did the book perhaps come from an estate?

I can't get over this possibility. Somehow, I'd still hoped for a decisive meeting. Was it already on the end-paper, has it already happened? You'd just be directed to eternal life again. Well, I bow my bald head.

MARKETPLACE

My pale muse, night creature, maybe a vampire, my pale Medusa, undersea secretary, always unsteady, but with burning kisses on the shinbone. Where do I escape from kisses and poems, the language wants everything, even whatever I don't want, from beautifully agitated mouths excuses fall into the clearest darkness. Beer is drunk there, and the conquerers stand on the platform, you dung-beetles, you pill-pushers of wisdom, and everything that exists is logical. Let us climb onto the gravestones and curse the secret servants!

I hate everybody, my button by the buttonhole, but we are only for nouns and prepositions. There's the ego in every line, it hides best. Hey there, and you won't find me, not me and not us. My muse is made of sand, my Medusa a stone that keeps looking out, my poster a shop sign that doesn't attract attention: Shoe Repair, End of Summer Sale, Sweets.

So we travel without companions, without a vehicle. Some think they have us, but already we've slipped away, under the sea, under the night, under the personal pronouns. There we look out, hedgehog and dormouse, joyful, peevish, sympathetic, we see fences and the sandfleas behind the grocery stores.

CARRYING BAG

Stores for candy
and spirits,
warehouses full of vinegar,
railroad crossings
and barberries,
the lines of verse from Zermatt
worn out with age,
badly packed,
and with every purchase
days fall out of your pocket,
and the *neige d'antan*
hangs in a shoeshape,
so the shopkeepers whisper
and an apprentice sniggers
behind the cabbage barrel.

PREAMBLE

Moles are what I write, their white claws turned out, the balls of their toes are pink, enjoyed by all their enemies as delicatessen, their thick coat prized. My moles are faster than you think. If you think they're over where the rotten wood and stone fly up, they're already off in their tunnels chasing down a thought. You could film their speed electronically by sticking some blades of grass down through. They're always a few meters ahead of all the other noses. Hey, we're over here, they could yell, but then they'd only feel sorry for the hare. My moles are destructive, don't fool yourselves. The grass over their tunnels dies off, of course they help it along. Traps are set, and they run right in blind. Some of them fling rats in the air. Wear us as lining for your coats, we're coat fodder, all of them think.

WINTER STUDENT AND
DAUGHTER-SON

My moles are washed and combed daily. A trained employee takes care of that, a winter student, 30, with her fourteen-year-old hermaphroditic child. In vain I have tried to hire a sodomite; they exist only in psychoanalytic reports and in the Old Testament. I am very pleased with the winter student, in the evenings she learns yoga technique, then in the summer she wants to take the exams in India. That's strange enough for the moles, they don't like stewardesses.

The winter student is dependent on demonstrations of love of all kinds. For a quarter of an hour a day I have to tickle the soles of her feet.

More, she says. She sleeps entwined with her daughter, often I look in helplessly, and am glad I'm not a master of the Indian techniques. My winter student has blue hair that contrasts well with the mole fur. She is good-natured, but only speaks faulty German. She knows no other languages, it's hereditary. Her son speaks a bit of Tibetan, perhaps from his father. His hair is red with black streaks, I don't understand anything about the laws of genetics.

Yes, I say to my winter student, she still understands that best. You are beautiful, I say, but that's already more difficult, she stretches out the sole of her foot to me. Several moles come climbing near, enthusiastically, the daughter mutters in Tibetan. You have blue hair, I say impressively, and she grabs for the bath soap, most of my sentences don't interest her.

It's hard to think about the summer. The moles are getting melancholy, and I don't know how to cheer them up. Moles depend on demonstrations of love, too, and I'm not clever enough for that, particularly since there are now over fifty, all distinctly marked.

Often I cross my legs, the only thing I automatically understand about yoga technique, and meditate. But without results.

INSIGHT

Everyone knows
that Mexico is an imaginary country.

As I opened the kitchen cupboard
I found the truth
hidden
in labeled canisters.

The rice grains
are resting up from the centuries.
Beyond the window
the wind continues on its way.

MAGIC SPELLS

Because—and already I falter, there are al-
ways reasons. Because the pictures hang
crooked, I wanted to say, but I don't continue
the sentence. Because I was born, oh sometime
or other. Really, you can omit the main clauses,
they don't go far, don't even go near.

The tulips turn to the wall, perhaps just to this
wall, just these tulips, it's abnormal. Because
the pictures hang crooked, but that's how every-
thing is connected, you feel yourself classified,
leg to leg, we all come from Merseburg.

Even the raven in the courtyard of the castle, later other cities too, Wessobrunn, which is really a village. The raven stole and a servant was executed, an accident, a connection. No one understands why subsequent ravens do penance for it, but it's customary.

Now it's noon, because the bells ring, because the sun is at its highest point, all these arrangements. It's good that it's noon, that finally gets us to the afternoon. School's out and you can eat barley soup, two bowls if you like. In other places other soups, somewhere even young ravens, they're supposed to taste like pheasants.

Meanwhile, Thor and Wotan are riding to the wood, in all kinds of weather, from all kinds of dwellings. They leave the tulips on the wall, the pictures crooked, everything sets itself right, like the foot of their horse. We are left behind, at best we can step just outside the door and listen for a ringing, for nothing, it simply comes to us, finally, because we were born, oh sometime or other.

REMAINDER

The minutes gone pale,
the ones I still have for dreaming,
ordering a strychnine pill at the counter,
obeying your eyes.
I can leave and return
to the pattern of your blouse,
it'll be long after the twilight
settles over the ship lights.
Let's go! The bills
have been written,
there's dust coming out of the trumpets.

BEETHOVEN, WOLF, AND SCHUBERT

Ah and Oh are two poems everyone under-
stands. And relatively short, they can be read
without long years of practice. Whether every-
one likes them is another matter, they don't hold
up if you expect some divine spark. Bravo or
encore encore would be so much better, but not
as short. In any case, sadness leads to anarchy,
it's that simple. Overjoyed, the wolf devours
his leg that's been torn off by a trap. Praised be
the day that gave me food, he cries. The wolf
should be an example to us. A tabula rasa is bet-
ter than an empty table, I thought of it from the
fabula rasa, the world is a misprint.

That shouldn't discourage us. What you need to live, you learn in every trap, and for cybernetics there are specially trained people. Or geometry—it follows automatically: while sitting, you can arrive at adjacent angles within parallels, if you try; sleeping is called 180 degrees; sorting potatoes leads to right angles. The world is a harmonious institution too, whether we know it or not. Franz Schubert slept with his glasses on, even that's all right, and when they get bent the optician fixes them. For the worst cases I've found a medicine, a kind of whiskey with yoga, little green pills which help for and against everything, above all for everything they help against. Everyone knows how important that is. My discovery, my contribution to the State. I rest on these laurels.

SIN

I'm no stranger to the temptation of the flesh.
I confess that I give in almost daily (except on
Fridays, when we have fish)—black butcher's
sausage, a little breakfast goulash.

In my butcher's garden, the sausage skins
float on a stake like balloons. Bewildering.
Intestines, cleaned of course, and almost trans-
parent. Well done. I read in a book on animal
theology that the task of man should be to turn
all the animals into house pets. What opportun-
ities! But whose?

So I go by my butcher's garden every day, and not counting the theological reflections, I think every day for eight minutes, that is to say all the way to the train station, trying to discover the Universal Mother's first name. I've already spent an incredible amount of time on this question, if I care to add it up. I've been going to the station for ten years, and three names have finally crystallized: Ellfrihde, Walltraut, and Ingeburck. Ten more years and I'll know which one is right.

Please wait for my results, before you make any hasty decisions on your own. As for the family name, we can all think about that one—there must be something Phoenician about it, like the first names.

NEW POSTCARDS

1

Melancholy trucks and
restaurants I don't believe in.
O sweet leaves of fall
and the wind
through Slovenian rooms.

2

Thanks, but leave us.
We've been in
the ratcatchers' caves already.

3

Or, river of mine, I can
explain you: source and tributaries,
my morning winnings, my restlessness,
my hourglass over all the countries.

4

It's mills I miss here.
The water's lazy,
the wind sticks.
It's time for steamroller works,
or clay pits
and burning barns,
hats for
the tenant farmers.

5

Surinam and the caterpillars.
Remember, Merian
Maria Sibylla,
I was the bent right
leaf on the carnation.

6

Here too the cat is waiting
in the grass for her bird.
We always thought the earthquakes
were a slamming door.
The children turn gray.

7

Oh huntersgreen, dolphindays,
the maple floors,
translated into feeling.

Agreed,
so let's read
the instructions for survivors.

8

Palmyra
is a squabble over tips,
father-in-law, son-in-law,
the surface goes into the earth,
a deposit of volatile Hölderlin,
the right attributes,
because he wasn't there,
no explanations
that wear you out.

9

A sick snow
and in footbaths,
the soluble patients—
lift me up
for the next-to-last office hour,
when the decisive winds
recite their long poems.

CHANGE OF CLIMATE

The door's probably open. Waiters, doctors, thieves, and tourists can walk in. The only possible way to keep people from coming into the room is to put money in front of the door. I've been doing it a long time. Only a cat still shows up. Later a sparrow hawk. He sees that he's got the wrong room number, and waves his arms helplessly. "48," I say, he thanks me and leaves. I sit a while in bed, maybe I was wrong, wasn't it 32? To tell the truth, I only know that it's an even number.

I want to get up and follow him, notice again that I stick to my sheets, the fear of choking begins again. At one time there had to be knobs on the air conditioners, 100 or 150 years ago, when the air tube was still open too. I wouldn't even know how to work it, if there were knobs. I don't know how anything is done, life, thanking people, meetings, how people see ballets and hear drums, and Meckel's graphics: Must you see them, must you hear them, touch them with your fingers? I have three senses, I'm only a glue to keep the sheets together, in a sheet I didn't want. When it gets light, in nine or ten hours, they'll wash me out. Good morning, I'll say.

MUNCH, CONSUL SANDBERG

The possibility
that the world is composed of colors
fills me with contempt.
I wish I had invented ice
and the boiling point
of metals.
Look at me:
I stand on your canvas
a nightmare of confidence
success in trouserlegs
and pointed boots;
the comedies of death
are played for my amusement.
In my mouth
I've got spit
for your hopes.

NATHANAEL

No one sees the man who rides on my shoulder. He has boneless serpentine legs, and tightens them around my neck if I do something he doesn't like. So I never go to the theater.

One day the bell rang and he was lying outside the door. Pick me up, he wailed, and at once, you might say suddenly, he sat on my shoulder when I bent down.

In The Thousand and One Nights a method for getting rid of shoulder-riders is given. You get drunk and make him envious, he wants to drink too, then you throw him off. But we've both become drunkards without his lessening the muscular pressure around my neck. We sing together and share our melancholy. Oh vile world, he says, and squeezes his legs even harder. If you let me fall, you'll get asthma, I know your old tricks.

He maintains his name is Nathanael, and offers to let me use the familiar. But I address him in the third person, as old Fritz did to his miller. If he doesn't want to get off, I have to go through a lot of doorways. But he just giggles, doors mean nothing to him. If I run into walls, I only hurt myself. Persuasion doesn't work, he has no moral feelings. Two times two is five, he says when he looks over my shoulder at the office, and embarrasses me. I must do everything wrong, otherwise he chokes me.

How long will he stay? I ask as calmly as possible. I have a good view here, he says, you're 1.97 meters tall. Should I be proud that he likes me best? I seek the company of tall people. That man there is two meters five, I say. No, he says, he's not right. Why am I the right one? I hope you'll never see, says Nathanael, shutting his eyes and yawning. Does he want to go to sleep now? Don't get your hopes up, he says.

LITTLE DAUGHTER

1

Catch the years
with lassos made of crocheted yarn,
darkened, all webbed together—
the tongue of the wolf, blue
dress of Mary, the
relationship to your teacher,

intricate years,
years spent reading, webbed together
and darkened,
correspondence in the snow,
paper plates for bees,

and down your back I follow
the lines in books,
the crocheted lines—
O Fallada, my horse,
my little goose feather, my flower,—
the lassos that have been retrieved.

2

But when
do we put our hands in our lap?
When will they come back from Cologne,
from the silvermines,
the valley of the Acherloo?
All those who screamed then:
who's eaten, eaten, drunk?
The people you put a wicker chair out for
by the stitches of air no one counted,
and beds of water and moss kettles?
The people who hold your mirror
three times the day after tomorrow,
who's the fairest of them all?

3

Miriam's built me a house
of bananas and oilcloth.
I'll stay there,
wait for everything there,
Scrabble and the shortness of breath,
sailor's chowder and every
other dish, every judgment,
even the Last.

KEY FIGURE

Lazy but brown, she can only be discussed in telegrams. I always see her going down the Avenue of September 19th to the bridge, which she doesn't cross. The woman from Wallachia wearing her borrowed fur with nothing underneath, you can read about it in the fairy tale, too lazy to spin herself material for a shift. Why is it called September 19th? I go to the post office to send my telegrams, coming back I never see her, she probably stays down by the bridge and turns into another person every day. I must stay until September 19th, to find a clue to the date, they're assembling down by the bridge, women from Wallachia, fur and nothing underneath, lazy and brown, and I send my telegrams until September 19th. The addressee knows the key, but the woman I've invented, she's there every day, I break out in sweat in front of the post office and I'm afraid to push the telegrams too far. To change the key, to touch the skin under the fur? There are means enough, but I would miss the Wallachian, the street down to the bridge, to the 19th of September. She's caught up with me, she's ahead of me by one reality.

DEFINITIVE

And let the snow
come through the door-cracks,
the wind blows, that's his job.

And let Lena be forgotten,
a girl who drank
the spirits from the lamp.

Went into the il-
lustrations of Meyer's Lexicon,
Brehm's Wildlife.

Intestines, mountainranges, beach carrion,
and let the snow
come through the door-cracks

up to the bed, up to the spleen,
where the memory sits,
where Lena sits,

the leopard, the feverish gull,
arithmetic puzzles in yellow
wrappers, by subscription.

And let the wind blow
because that's all he can do
and don't begrudge Lena

one more swig from the lamp
and let the snow
come through the door-cracks.

LAURAS

If there is no Laura, there is still her name. She has small ears which are hidden by her curls, that you can be sure of. The color of her hair is uncertain, but red would be surprising. There is less literature about Laura than about William Tell. That's a shame. I could talk better with

Laura than with Petrarch, who wanted to repeat everything, only more beautifully. A false artistic principle, but we want that too. What did Eve say, what did Bathsheba say, what did Noah say when he deserted his friends in the rain? Nobody knows, but we want to say it finally. Nobody knows Laura, but let's invent her now. She plays the piano. Since her inner life longs for expression, probably too loudly. Her eye is fixed on a point beyond all pianos—now we're getting somewhere. I dare say she's a captain's widow. Young, but a woman whom suffering has matured. Now we know more. But more beautiful. Laura's getting more and more beautiful. A beauty-mark, a lily neck, a very narrow waist. At once she comes to life and plays the piano. Beset by admirers, she uses up her meager widow's pension. Francesco and Friedrich are her favorites. Francesco stays, later Friedrich turns to a Caroline and a Charlotte. She suffers and outlives both. Died in 1899 in the Tropical Institute of the University of Tübingen. If we know her death, we know everything. Death, my principal, says Friedrich, most powerful czar of all flesh.

BRICKWORKS BETWEEN 1900 AND 1910

1

Don't think back
over the bricks,
the wintering, blue tinges.
The measurements have survived
among the farmers,
a kind of legend
that holds you from a distance,
a family of knowledge,
fruitful, astonished,
the ingenious
memory built into
overgrown ovens:
A horse
won in the lottery,
the brickmaker's sister,
winter workman,
something written in
indelible pencil
on the paving stones
of the stable passageway.

2

Stone loaves
shot through with air
soured by rain—
nobody's hunger,
nobody's red bread.
Grab the plains!
time belongs to the clay pits,
a sour rain, a trace of
caraway, rinds
from pictures.

3

Unbalanced budget.
A year of defective tiles.
Who can break even
in this short life
when the limbs
swell up with water
and you look helplessly
at the tar-covered trellises,
at the canaries
that die carelessly
in the closing door?

4

Icelandic moss,
a word whispered
in hearing tests
understood
from two meters.

A precise dryness
behind the Wendic graves,
a region that becomes
audible under
the paws of a mongrel.

A precise
Icelandic
regional word, all that
is nothing but future Wendic
moss
among us dogs,
among us graves
audibly grayed
dry whispering pawed.

5

Dachshunds,
a huge white horse,
the brick that grows resonant.

Rhubarb in the Garden of Eden,
furious outbursts from peacocks,
round-ovens.

Bibup, the teacher from the next village,
being sick,
an automobile.

SOME REMARKS ON "LITERATURE AND REALITY"

All the views that have been presented here assume that we know what reality is. I have to say for myself that I do not know. That we have all come here to Vézelay, this room, this green tablecloth, all this seems very strange to me and hardly real.

We know there are colors we do not see, sounds we do not hear. Our senses are uncertain, and I must assume my brain is too. I suspect our discomfort with reality lies in what we call time. I find it absurd that the moment I am saying this already belongs to the past. I am incapable of accepting reality as it presents itself to us as reality.

On the other hand, I do not wish to play the fool who does not know he has bumped into a table. I am prepared to orient myself in this room. But I have the same sort of difficulties that a deaf and dumb blind man has.

Well, all right. My existence is an attempt of this kind: to accept reality sight unseen. Writing is also possible in these terms, but I am trying to write something that aims in another direction—I mean the poem.

I write poems to orient myself in reality. I view them as trigonometric points or buoys that mark the course in an unknown area. Only through writing do things take on reality for me. Reality is my goal, not my presupposition. First I must establish it.

I am a writer. Writing is not only a profession but also a decision to see the world as language. Real language is a falling together of the word and the object. Our task is to translate from the language that is around us but not "given." We are translating without the original text. The most successful translation is the one that gets closest to the original and reaches the highest degree of reality.

I must admit that I have not come very far along in this translating. I am still not beyond the "thing-word" or noun. I am like a child that says "tree," "moon," "mountain" and thus orients himself.

Therefore, I have little hope of ever being able to write a novel. The novel has to do with the verb, which in German is rightly called the "activity word." But I have not penetrated the territory of the verb. I shall still need several decades for the "thing-word" or noun.

Let us use the word "definition" for these

trigonometric signs. Such definitions are not only useful for the writer but it is absolutely necessary that he set them up. In each good line of poetry I hear the cane of the blindman striking: I am on secure ground now.

I am not saying that the correctness of definitions depends on the length or brevity of texts. A novel of four hundred pages is likely to contain as many "definitions" as a poem of four lines. I would consider such a novel a poem.

Correctness of definition and literary quality are identical for me. Language begins where the translation approaches the original. What comes before this may be psychologically, sociologically, politically or any-cally interesting, and I shall gladly be entertained by it, admire it and rejoice in it, but it is not *necessary*. The poem alone is *necessary* for me.